Praise for …

CRAZY LOVE

"Chan writes with infectious exuberance, challenging Christians to take the Bible seriously. He describes at length the sorry state of 'lukewarm' Christians who strive for a life characterized by control, safety, and an absence of suffering. In stark contrast, the book offers real-life accounts of believers who have given all—time, money, health, even their lives—in obedience to Christ's call. Chan also recounts his own attempts to live 'crazy' by significantly downsizing his home and giving away his resources to the poor. Earnest Christians will find valuable take-home lessons from Chan's excellent book."

Publishers Weekly

"In Francis Chan's unique style, and with an urgency that seeks to awaken a sleeping church mired in the comfort of middle ground, *Crazy Love* quickly gets to the heart of the matter and leaves you wanting more … more of the matchless Jesus who offers radical life for all right now."

Louie Giglio, visionary architect, director of Passion Conferences, and author of *I Am Not, but I Know I AM*

"Francis's life reflects authentic leadership tempered by a deep compassion for the lost, the last, the littlest, and the least. It's all because this man, my friend, is an ardent and devoted disciple of his Savior. In his fresh new book, *Crazy Love*, Francis peels back what we think the Christian life is, and guides us down the path toward an uncommon intimacy with Jesus—an intimacy which can't help but change the world around us!"

Joni Eareckson Tada, best-selling author and speaker

"In an age of religious phonies, spiritual apathy, and disheartening books suggesting that God is a delusion, *Crazy Love* shines like a glorious beacon of hope and light. If you're stuck in a religious rut, read this refreshing book. I found it eye-opening and soul-thrilling. Whether in the pulpit or on the page, Francis Chan effuses love for Jesus Christ and demonstrates practical ways to throw off lukewarm Christianity and embrace full-on, passionate love for God."

Kirk Cameron, actor and author of *Still Growing*

living

↓↑

crazy love

living ↓↑ crazy love

AN INTERACTIVE WORKBOOK FOR
INDIVIDUAL OR SMALL-GROUP STUDY

FRANCIS CHAN
and Mark Beuving

David C Cook®

transforming lives together

LIVING CRAZY LOVE
Published by David C Cook
4050 Lee Vance View
Colorado Springs, CO 80918 U.S.A.

David C Cook Distribution Canada
55 Woodslee Avenue, Paris, Ontario, Canada N3L 3E5

David C Cook U.K., Kingsway Communications
Eastbourne, East Sussex BN23 6NT, England

The graphic circle C logo is a registered trademark of David C Cook.

The website addresses recommended throughout this book are offered as a resource to you. These websites are not intended in any way to be or imply an endorsement on the part of David C Cook, nor do we vouch for their content.

Scripture taken from *The Holy Bible, English Standard Version*. Copyright © 2000; 2001 by Crossway Bibles, a division of Good News Publishers. Used by permission. All rights reserved.

LCCN 2011932485
ISBN 978-1-4347-0387-3
eISBN 978-1-4347-0466-5

Published in association with the literary agency of
D.C. Jacobson & Associates LLC, an Author Management Company
www.dcjacobson.com

The Team: Don Pape, Karen Lee-Thorp, Amy Kiechlin Konyndyk, Nick Lee, Caitlyn York, Karen Athen.
Cover Design: Jim Elliston, The Regime

Printed in the United States of America

First Edition 2011

4 5 6 7 8 9 10

111011

CONTENTS

GETTING STARTED

Would you say that your life is characterized by love? Love for God? Love for the people around you? Or is there something else that drives you? We'd probably all be quick to affirm that we love God and love the people around us. But how many of us could really say that we are *driven* by love?

The Christian life is as simple and as difficult as this profound statement: "God is love, and whoever abides in love abides in God, and God abides in him" (1 John 4:16). That's it. Abide in love. Greater than any self-help strategy or formula for achieving happiness is this powerful call to simply love. It sounds easy enough, right?

I suppose love would be easy if we could define it any way we'd like. But at the heart of the biblical concept of love is a God who demonstrated His love by making the supreme sacrifice: "God shows his love for us in that while we were still sinners, Christ died for us" (Rom. 5:8). When you put it like that, love doesn't seem so easy. Add to that Jesus' statement in John 14:15: "If you love me, you will keep my commandments." Clearly love is far more important, far less fluffy, and far more involved than we tend to think.

Our lives should be characterized by love. First, we should be absolutely transformed by the love of God. Most of us need to radically expand our view of God's love. Have you ever sat in awe as you considered the fact that the Creator of the universe—the God who spoke the world into existence, the God who conquered sin and death by bursting forth from the grave, the God who will ultimately set the world to rights and to whom every single knee will bow—that *this* God *loves you?*

I don't hesitate to say that if we truly grasped the improbability and overwhelming power of God's love, we would be changed forever. We would think differently. Feel differently. Live differently. Nothing would be the same.

Probably the biggest change would come in the form of our love for God. What do you suppose an appropriate response to God's love looks like? Should you do a bunch of good things so you can pay Him back? Should you try to stay out of trouble so He doesn't have to worry about you anymore? Or should you continue to pursue His love and allow it to transform you and everyone you come into contact with?

This study is meant to help you think through God's intense, relentless love and how that love should transform every aspect of your being. The thoughts and questions addressed in the following pages will help you to examine your life and take important steps toward pursuing God. *Living Crazy Love* is about growing into a wholehearted devotion to God.

When Paul prayed for the Ephesian churches, he asked God to strengthen them so they could comprehend the incomprehensible love of God (Eph. 3:14–19). My prayer for you is the same. God's love changes everything, and I want nothing more for you than that you would understand God's love and respond appropriately. Never forget that we love because He first loved us (1 John 4:19).

HOW TO GET THE MOST OUT OF THIS WORKBOOK

There are a few different ways to use this workbook. You can work through the study as an individual, as a part of a small group, or even during a weekend retreat. I've made some suggestions for using the workbook in each of these settings below.

This workbook is designed to work hand in hand with the *Crazy Love* book and the *Crazy Love DVD Study Resource*. Ideally, you will read the relevant chapter from *Crazy Love,* then go through the corresponding session in the workbook, watching the appropriate video from the DVD when prompted.

But while that is the most thorough way of studying the material, the workbook also stands on its own. You'll notice that each session refers to the book and the DVD, but you can get a lot out of this workbook without those resources.

USING THE WORKBOOK ON YOUR OWN

The most effective way to use this workbook is to go through it on your own, even if you're also going to discuss it as a group or on a retreat. Many of the questions are personal, and taking the time to read through the sessions and think through how each question should affect your life will give the study depth and immediate personal application.

If you have the *Crazy Love* book, I suggest reading the corresponding chapter before starting each session of the workbook. If you have the *Crazy Love DVD Study Resource,* you'll notice that each session prompts you to watch the appropriate video at a particular point in the study. I recommend watching the video when prompted and then working through the rest of the session.

USING THE WORKBOOK IN A SMALL GROUP

If you're working through the material as a part of a small group, the best way to begin is by working through each chapter on your own before the group discussion (see the section for individuals above). Reading and thinking through each session on your own before your group meets will better prepare you for the discussion. I recommend writing in your answers and any notes or questions you may have before you meet with your group and then adding to your notes based on the discussion.

When you meet with your group, I recommend establishing a discussion leader. (If you've been chosen for this task, see the "Notes for Discussion Leaders" at the end of this workbook.) This person doesn't need to have all the answers. The discussion leader will simply guide the conversation and decide when to move on to the next question.

For each session, discuss the numbered questions as a group. I suggest jumping from one question to the next, but feel free to read a section out loud if the questions are unclear. Some of the questions can be answered quickly, but I encourage you to take your time, giving multiple group members a chance to share. This will enrich the discussion, and different perspectives will often give you more ideas for practical application.

At a specific point in each session, you will be prompted to play the *Crazy Love DVD Study Resource*. I suggest getting one copy for your group and watching the videos together while you meet. If you do it this way, individual group members will work through the material on their own and wait to watch the videos until the group meets. When you get together, discuss the numbered questions until you are prompted to watch the DVD. After the video, discuss the rest of the questions.

It may be helpful to arrange chairs in a U shape around the television so that everyone can see the screen when you watch the video and so that everyone can see other's faces as you discuss your thoughts before and after the video. If this arrangement is possible, then you won't need to move chairs during your meeting.

Most importantly, I encourage you to be honest with the members of your group. If your desire is to grow and change, you will need the other group members to pray for you, support you, and at times challenge your thinking. By opening up to one another, your whole group will become more open to the Spirit's leading.

USING THE WORKBOOK FOR A WEEKEND RETREAT

Some churches will want to use this workbook as a part of a weekend retreat. If that's the case, the retreat leaders have some decisions to make: Do you want to use the *Crazy Love DVD Study Resource* for all or some of the main sessions? Maybe you'll want to plan out messages around the material covered in each session (if that's the case, I highly recommend reading the *Crazy Love* book). You may just want to plan out meeting times during the course of the weekend, play the DVD for the whole group, and then have everyone break off into smaller groups to discuss the material.

Ten meetings (one per session) are a lot for one weekend. If you have to select just five or seven, go for it. Think it through, though, because the sessions do build from one to the next. Encourage people to read the chapters you're skipping (they're not long). And do include session 10, because people need to walk away with a plan to do something, even something small.

However you choose to do it, I recommend dividing the large group into smaller groups for discussion. Small groups of four to six people give everyone a chance to talk. People who are shy about talking in large groups are often more comfortable talking in small ones. And people who tend to dominate discussions in large groups are more easily balanced out by others in small circles. It's a good idea for people to stick with the same group for the whole series, so that they get to know each other.

You'll probably want to address the entire group at least a few times during the weekend to give them some thoughts, but giving them time to meet in smaller groups will be important. Group members will want to read the section for small groups above, and discussion leaders will want to read the "Notes for Discussion Leaders" section at the end of this workbook.

Discussion leaders don't need to be experts either in the content or in leading groups, because they will fairly quickly learn how to guide a conversation with only four to six other people. Ideally, you will choose discussion leaders ahead of time, but if you can't, it's surprising how often these groups can choose the most natural leader among them after getting to know one another for only a brief time. You can read aloud the job description of a discussion leader (see the end of this workbook) and pray for the Holy Spirit to guide the groups in choosing discussion leaders. Groups will often unanimously choose someone among them to do the job once they know what it involves.

Because small groups may be scattered around your meeting area with chairs in small circles, you'll need to decide when and how to watch the video together. It takes time and organization if people have to stop their discussion, move from one location to another, watch the video, and then move back to their discussion circle. Because the video is brief, you may find that, with a large group, the easiest plan is to view the video all together at the beginning of each meeting period and then scatter the small groups for discussion for the rest of the period.

STOP PRAYING

For more information on the material in this session, read the Preface and chapter 1 of the book *Crazy Love: Overwhelmed by a Relentless God.*

If you have the *Crazy Love DVD Study Resource,* watch the video for session 1 now, particularly if you are meeting with a group. After the video, work through the rest of this session.

One of the most frightening aspects of the Christian life is that we can actually become apathetic about speaking to *God!* This isn't about getting bored while talking to an economics professor, an old friend, or even your spouse—we have the privilege of talking to God through prayer, and yet most of us pray regularly without thinking about what we're doing. I'm convinced that our relationships with God would be absolutely transformed if we all took the simple step of considering who God is.

Even though you're just beginning this session, stop right now. Take a few minutes to actually consider who it is you're talking to. Then write down some thoughts in response to the two questions below.

1. **What do you think would come out of your mouth the moment you first saw God? What would be the first words you would say?**

    Thank you
    Sorry

2. **How has your relationship with God and your prayer life been different as a result of reading chapter 1 and considering God's glory? If your life hasn't been different enough, how would you like to see it change?**

Prayer is a unique privilege. We actually get to come before God, enjoy His presence, and ask Him to work in our lives. Yet I'm amazed at how quickly I forget the significance of prayer. I often approach prayer as a given and halfheartedly throw my requests at God without giving it (or God) a second thought.

Solomon has some heavy words for those of us who are quick to rush into God's presence:

Guard your steps when you go to the house of God. To draw near to listen is better than to offer the sacrifice of fools, for they do not know that they are doing evil. Be not rash with your mouth, nor let your heart be hasty to utter a word before God, for God is in heaven and you are on earth. Therefore let your words be few. (Eccl. 5:1–2)

We have a tendency to rush into God's presence irreverently—speaking our mind and rarely stopping to enjoy His presence or consider what He may want to say to us. I can't say that I ever consciously developed my prayer life, but I can tell you that I didn't build my prayer life around an appropriate view of God. I grew up praying because I was told to do so; my prayer habits were deeply entrenched before I stopped to consider what I was actually doing.

Take some time to pause and think through two things. First, spend some time meditating on Solomon's words. What is he getting at? Why is he saying this? How would your life look different if you made these words fundamental to your approach to God? After you've thought this through for a bit, analyze the way you pray: when you pray, how often, what you ask for, how you address God, etc. When you're ready, continue with the questions below.

3. **Describe your prayer life. Do you find yourself talking *at* God, or do you take time to consider who you are talking to and enjoy being awed by His presence? Why do you think you tend to pray the way you do?**

Inherent in Solomon's argument is an incredibly high view of God. If God is exactly like us, then we may not see the need to approach Him with a sense of awe. But if God is who He says He is, then Solomon's words are especially poignant: Only fools rush into the presence of God.

4. How often do you stop to consider how great God is and how insignificant you are by comparison? When you do, what leads you to this point? If you never do, why do you think you've never done this?

5. How can you build these times of reflection into your lifestyle?

Perhaps you're convinced at this point. Maybe all you needed was a reminder of God's greatness, and everything you've been reading has reinspired you to view God in all His glory. Even if that's the case, you still have many obstacles to overcome—not just now, but on an ongoing basis. It's all but impossible to escape the incessant distractions in our lives. There are so many things—many of them good things—that keep us from thinking about that which is most important in life.

Take some time to think about your specific lifestyle and context. Think about what this sort of awareness of God's greatness would look like as a part of your daily life.

6. What things in your life distract you from loving and worshipping God the way He deserves to be loved and worshipped?

What can you do to overcome these obstacles?

In addition to the obstacles and distractions we all face, there is a more subtle and potent aspect of our lives that would keep us from living in light of God's absolute greatness. Even if we believe that God is greater than we are, we all have to overcome our tendency to view God as an all-powerful genie. In other words, it's possible to view God as powerful but to misunderstand His purpose, to believe that God exists to grant our wishes and make us happy.

This is an extremely important concept to explore. When you think about the whole point of the universe, do you see God at the center of everything? Or do you see yourself and your happiness as the ultimate goal? Try to move beyond your intellectual answer and analyze your emotions and core commitments. And don't stop there. Examine your life and consider what your lifestyle might reveal about this. What do your priorities and actions say about the way you view God?

7. **Which aspects of your priorities, thoughts, and actions declare that you exist for God's service and glory?**

8. **Which aspects of your life declare that God exists for your benefit and service?**

9. **If there are aspects of your life that declare that God exists for your benefit and service, how can you begin to reorder these aspects of your life around the reality of God's greatness and your dependence on Him?**

I think the best way to end this session is to push you to stand in the presence of God. In just a minute, I'm going to ask you to read Revelation 4. In this passage, John finds himself standing in the throne room of heaven. His language and tone reveal that he is not prepared for what he sees. Everything about John's vision is stunning: the physical layout of the throne room, the flashing lightning and roaring thunder, the bizarre creatures before the throne and their strong response to God's glory, and especially the picture of God Himself seated on the throne.

Read this passage, and try to imagine yourself standing where John stood and watching this scene unfold. It may seem fanciful, but John is describing reality. As you place yourself in the midst of Revelation 4, allow yourself to experience all of the surprise and awe that John must have experienced. After you've spent some time reading and thinking about this passage, continue below.

10. **Which details in this passage strike you the most? Why?**

Recalling the scene in Revelation 4 would be a great place to start before you pray. But there are many other things you can do to remind yourself of God's greatness. Maybe it's stepping out under the stars and considering the immense size of God's creation, or meditating on the greatness of God's love for you, or considering the intricate design of the human body. Whatever it is, we should be reminded of God's greatness on a regular basis. This is His world after all, and it is literally shouting about His greatness at every moment (see Psalm 19).

But even though reminders of God's greatness are all around us, we still need to pay attention to them. We still need to develop a habit of noticing God's glory and reminding ourselves of why He's so great.

11. What can you do right now to ensure that you will pause before every prayer to consider the God you are praying to?

12. Spend some time in prayer. Before you begin speaking, however, put into practice some of the realities you've been considering. Take time to picture God on His throne. Consider the angels shouting about His holiness and the twenty-four elders throwing their crowns at His feet as they fall on their faces. After you've taken some time to remind yourself of who God is and to enjoy the greatness of His presence, then begin talking to Him. But even then, heed Solomon's warning, and let your words be few.

STOP PRAYING

YOU MIGHT NOT FINISH THIS CHAPTER

For more information on the material in this session, read chapter 2 of the book *Crazy Love: Overwhelmed by a Relentless God.*

Do you want to make an impact on your world? There's no way you're going to answer that question negatively. Some are more consciously driven by this goal than others, but we all want to make a difference; we all want to influence people for good.

But if this is what we're all striving for, why do we seem to get stuck in a rut of mediocrity? I'm not suggesting that if you're not a missionary or a millionaire, then your life doesn't matter. I'm simply saying that we all get caught up doing things that don't really matter. We all get distracted. And I think we all know this is the case. We want something more. We long to make a difference, to devote ourselves to something bigger and better.

Sadly, most of us have been taught to settle. We've come to accept that the Christian life is about being somewhat moral, attending a church service, and saying our prayers. But we all know this is shallow. We were meant to live for a much greater purpose than personal comfort. Christianity is about taking broken people, transforming them, and then using those transformed people to transform the world. It's always been this way, from the moment when the Holy Spirit came upon the early church in Acts 2.

So what keeps you from pursuing greatness? What holds you back from seeking everything God wants for you and is calling you to? My suspicion is that most Christians settle for less simply because they get busy and distracted with so many other things. Of course, there are many distractions in our lives that shouldn't be there—I'm thinking here of actively engaging in sinful activities or pursuing things that God has clearly directed you away from. But there are many good things in our lives that also end up distracting us from pursuing the things we know God is calling us to.

Even things as good as jobs, kids, spouses, church programs, etc., can take our eyes off of what is most important if we begin to view them and use them in the wrong way. There is a healthy, appropriate, and incredibly important side to each of these good activities, and pouring huge amounts of time and energy into them may be the best way for you to serve God. But the subtle deception of idolatry pushes us to take that which is good and use it in ungodly ways. So while investing in our kids and teaching them to love God and serve the people around them would bring glory to God, our twisted desire to have perfect, high-achieving kids who make us look good in public would not.

1. **List the elements in your life that keep you distracted. Include both good things and bad things in this list.**

Once you have identified some of these things, it's important to evaluate why you got distracted in the first place. As I said, good things can take our attention off of the most important things. But why do these good things end up being distractions? God wants you to be diligent and creative in your job. If you're married, God wants you to devote time, attention, and love toward your spouse. If you have children, God wants you to invest time into their lives, loving them and teaching them how to function in the world that God created.

But if you find yourself so focused on these things that you aren't enjoying God's presence in the midst of it, consciously trying to honor God through the way you do these activities and pursuing the things that you know God wants you to pursue, then these things have become distractions. It's helpful to evaluate how these good things ended up pushing you in the wrong direction. By thinking this through, you will be setting yourself up to restructure your life in a way that does not neglect the good things that God has given you, but also allows you to stay focused on God's purpose for your life.

2. How is it that the good things in your life have come to distract you from what is most important?

3. What would it take to adjust your lifestyle and mentality in order to put the most important things back in their proper place?

It's incredibly important that we keep our lives in the proper perspective. For one thing, we go to great lengths to avoid thinking about death. We all know that life is fragile, but who wants to think about the end of their life? It's easy to get people to visualize wealth and success, but nobody wants to acknowledge that they could die today.

We also like to live as though we were the center of the universe. Most of us would deny this, but when we examine the way we spend our time and money, it sure looks like we are the kings of our own mini-kingdoms. Our lives are focused on our goals, our desires, and our decisions.

We know that we could die at any moment and that we're not really the center of the universe. But what does it take to put everything in the proper perspective—to see the world as God sees it?

Start by reading James 4:13–17. It's a short passage with a simple point. But don't read it too quickly. Take some time to meditate on what James is saying. After you've considered the passage for a while, continue by answering the questions below.

4. **Make a few notes on this passage. What is James warning against? What is he calling us to do?**

5. **If James were to say these words specifically to you in the midst of your current life situation, what do you think he would tell you to avoid? What do you think he would tell you to pursue?**

One telltale sign of misplaced priorities and a misunderstanding of your role in the universe is stress or anxiety. Of course, stress is a pervasive aspect of our modern culture. A "successful career" is just another way of referring to a stressful lifestyle. The more we are responsible for, the more we feel that weight and the more anxious we get.

Even though stress and anxiety are givens in our culture, a stressful lifestyle carries a certain amount of arrogance. It's not wrong to be appropriately busy, but it's wrong to be anxious about the things in our lives, as if we have control over how things will turn out. Even though Paul tells us to rejoice *always* (Phil. 4:4), we think that our circumstances are more important and that if we work hard enough, we can make everything turn out all right.

Getting rid of the anxiety in your life doesn't necessarily mean that you should quit your job or stop every activity that keeps you busy (though it may mean one or both of these things). You may well keep doing the exact same things you're doing now, but keeping everything in perspective is absolutely essential. And this means that you have to put even yourself in perspective. Again, we have to remember that we're not in control of our lives. We are absolutely dependent on God. We have a responsibility to act and obey God, but we're not going to change the world on our own by simply trying harder.

6.   What are the sources of stress and anxiety in your life?

It's easy to simply say, "Stop being anxious; just trust God." Unfortunately, that's often the council we give and receive when it comes to anxiety and stress. It's good advice to some extent: We do need to stop being anxious, and we do need to trust God. But what would that really look like in your life? Don't settle for an easy answer here—try to wrestle with this. Think about your proper place in the universe and the everyday situations that you find yourself in. Make some notes below to help you begin putting your stressful situations in the right perspective.

7. **What can you do to remind yourself of God's care and your dependence on Him in the midst of these stressful situations?**

The Christian life is all about dependence on God. Again, this is something that we'd probably all agree on, but most of our lives look more like demonstrations of our own independence than humble attempts to rely on God in every situation. If this is God's world, if every moment of your life is a gift from God, and if your life is about God's kingdom rather than your own, then those realities ought to be reflected in the way you live.

8. **How can you structure your life to reflect the fact that your every second is dependent on the grace of God?**

If you have the *Crazy Love DVD Study Resource*, watch the video for session 2 now, particularly if you are meeting with a group. After the video, work through the rest of this session.

Once we are reminded of our proper place in the universe, we can begin to function as God intended for us to function. Our lives will be off base and our priorities will be skewed unless we see ourselves as God sees us. Remember that this world is about God, not us. If we live for anything other than God's glory, we will end with regrets.

I'm reminded of the importance of this every time someone around me dies. It's actually healthy for us to be exposed to death from time to time. Solomon says this explicitly in Ecclesiastes 7. By remembering that our lives are fragile—that it could all be over at any moment—we'll find it easier to stay focused on the most important things in life.

9.   **Describe some people in your life who have died abruptly. What were some of their achievements in life and what were their regrets?**

10. **If today was the day you died, what would you regret, and why?**

11. **What can you change about your life today to avoid those regrets?**

12. **Close your time in this session by praying. You've been thinking through some pretty heavy issues, and if you're seriously thinking about making changes in your life to avoid regrets, you likely have some important changes to make. Remember that this life is all about dependence on God and that so many things will pull you away from His simple calling on your life. Spend some time asking God to work in your heart and mind to remove distractions and place you on the path He's calling you to.**

YOU MIGHT NOT FINISH THIS CHAPTER

CRAZY LOVE

For more information on the material in this session, read chapter 3 of the book *Crazy Love: Overwhelmed by a Relentless God.*

"Love the Lord your God with all your heart and with all your soul and with all your mind and with all your strength" (Mark 12:30). According to Jesus, this is the most important commandment in the Bible. Many people would point to good works, obedience, or devotion to doctrine as the heart of Christianity. Of course, these things are all important parts of the Christian life, but Jesus never identifies any of these things as most important. Instead, He points us to love for God.

We know that God loves us and that we should love God. But there is no way I would characterize most Christians or most churches by their love for God. People in love act much differently than people with a sense of obligation. People do crazy things for love. Love has a way of making even the most difficult tasks feel simple and joyful. It has a way of pushing us to act with complete abandon and devotion. If we were truly in love with God, then our lives would be shaped by God, His desires for us, and our desire to maintain a close relationship with Him.

I'm not suggesting that you simply try harder to conjure up more love for God. But I do think that if we took just a few minutes to contemplate God's amazing love for us, then our lives could be changed forever. When we begin to grasp even a hint of God's incredible love, the only possible response is complete love and devotion.

Every Christian knows God's love in an intellectual sense. That is, we could check the right box on a doctrinal exam. But this is much different from knowing God's love intimately. Our knowledge of God's love should penetrate to the core of our being. Not only should we acknowledge that God loves us, we should be able to identify ways in which God's love has changed us and created in us a passionate love for Him in return.

1. **How would you explain the difference between knowing God's love intellectually and knowing it intimately?**

    Which is your default when thinking about God's love? Why do you think this is the case?

The psalms say a lot about God's love. They cover a wide range of emotion, but it's not difficult to find psalms that praise God for His love in hyperbolic terms. The psalmists frequently recount God's love by pointing to the specific things God has done to show His love to His people. Consider these words from David:

> You have multiplied, O LORD my God,
>   your wondrous deeds and your thoughts toward us;
>   none can compare with you!
> I will proclaim and tell of them,
>   yet they are more than can be told. (40:5)

It's a very healthy exercise for all of us to pause from time to time and consider what God has done for us. Of course, our life experiences are varied, and we have all gone through dark times. But take some time to think about the gifts, events, relationships, and other blessings from God that show His love for you. I encourage you to take a significant amount of time here: Let God's blessings pile up in your mind, then answer the questions below.

2. **Think about your life and your relationship with God. How does God demonstrate His love to you? Be specific.**

How do these demonstrations of God's love affect you? (Don't think about how these things _ought to_ make you feel; describe how they _actually_ make you feel and what they move you to do.)

As soon as we start talking about our life circumstances, we face an important question: How do we reconcile our negative experiences with the fact that God loves us? Most of us don't have to dig very deep into our past before we uncover some event that would cause us to question God's love for us. It's important to view these experiences from the proper perspective and to allow God's truth to interpret events for us. But that doesn't mean we should stifle our questions or pretend that these things don't matter.

The same Bible that repeatedly tells us that God loves His people unconditionally records numerous accounts of bad things happening to good people. We would be foolish to pretend that bad things don't happen and that they don't affect us deeply. Take some time to think about the negative things that have happened to you and how those things have made you feel. Be honest if these things have made you question God's love. Addressing some of these issues is important for beginning to truly experience God's love for you.

3. **Describe some things that have made you question God's love for you (whether God gave you things you didn't want, didn't give you what you wanted, or took something good from you). How do these things make you feel about God and His love?**

Sometimes things look much different from our perspective than they must look from God's perspective. Paul says that we see the world "in a mirror dimly" (1 Cor. 13:12). He also says that we walk by faith, not by sight (2 Cor. 5:7). There is so much about the world and the events in our lives that we simply do not understand. If all we ever do is look at our circumstances, then we are bound to wonder sometimes whether God truly loves us. Sure, we all have many experiences that verify God's love for us. But if we're overwhelmed by the bad things that happen in our lives, we may wonder if God really is holding us in His loving arms.

When we read the Bible, however, there is no mistaking God's pervasive, relentless, unconditional love for us. Usually, the difference between God's Word and our experiences is a matter of perspective. Again, this doesn't mean that you should suppress your emotions and doubts. All I'm saying is that God's love for us is far more powerful than the negative events in our lives. It goes far deeper than our limited ability to perceive His love toward us. Our understanding of God's love must be more profound than the naive expectation of a carefree life.

As you process your life in light of the biblical promises of God's love, allow God to work on your heart. This begins with honestly opening yourself up to the scrutiny of God and His truth. Spend a few minutes considering your unique situation and contemplating God's unrelenting love in that context.

4. **In light of your circumstances, what would it mean to believe and embrace God's love for you?**

If you have the *Crazy Love DVD Study Resource,* watch the video for session 3 now, particularly if you are meeting with a group. After the video, work through the rest of this session.

There is a huge difference between obeying God out of duty and pursuing Him out of love. Of course, if you love God, you will ultimately obey Him (see John 14:15). But obeying God because you love Him and obeying Him because you're told you ought to are different things.

If you have ever experienced that moment of realizing that you actually love God, take some time to reflect on it. If you haven't gotten to that point, it's okay—that's why I'm pushing you to think through all of this. Also take some time to think about how you can help the other Christians in your life to remember God's love and the relationship He wants to have with each of us. Answer the questions below as you think this through.

5. Do you remember the moment when you "got it," when you first realized you loved God with your heart, mind, and soul? Describe that moment.

6. How can you work together with the Christians in your life to remind one another throughout the week of the love Jesus demonstrated on the cross?

Of all the biblical statements about God's love, none hit me as hard as Romans 8:31–39. There's something about Paul's clarity and passion in this section that inspires me. It's difficult for me to read Paul's words without getting either emotional or excited. Take a minute to read through this passage. As you do, allow Paul's words to hit you full force. Keep in mind that Paul was not talking about some distant God loving people who are now long dead. No, Paul was describing the God who is there with you as you read these words and the intense, unconditional love He has for you. Use the questions below to help you process the passage.

7. As you read this passage, what stands out to you about God's love for you?

8. **What bearing should this description of God's love have on the way you think about your relationship with God?**

The reality of God's love hits us even harder when we begin to see how important God is. If God is a helpful—or even necessary—addition to our lives as we pursue our hopes and dreams (wealth, fulfillment, fame, self-actualization, or whatever your life is devoted to), then the fact that God loves is nice, but not amazing. But if God is the greatest good in the universe, if everything in this world comes from Him and is ultimately all about Him and His glory, then God's love for us means everything. If God is important but not absolutely essential, then we will have to weigh our options about how and how much to love Him. But if He is the greatest being in the universe, then nothing matters more than God's love for us and our love for Him.

Most Christians would say that God is the highest good in the universe. But think about that statement for a while. Can you honestly say you believe that God is greater than any person, possession, career, or goal in the world? Can you say with complete integrity that He deserves every bit of your devotion, every ounce of your love, and every moment of your time? I'm not asking you whether your devotion to God is complete (Jesus is the only one who has ever done this perfectly); I'm asking whether you believe that God is worthy of your complete devotion. Take some time to seriously consider this question.

9. **In the past—or even right now—what would you have said the greatest good on earth is? (Be honest here—don't simply say, "God" because you know it's the right answer.)**

10. Can you honestly say that you believe God is the greatest good in the universe? If not, what keeps you from affirming this? If so, what makes Him the greatest good?

11. As you end this session, spend some time increasing your intimacy with God. You don't have to take a long time right now, but it's important to take some steps. You might do this by reading your Bible, praying, singing, or doing some other activity that helps you draw close to God. The important thing is that you purposefully draw close to Him and enjoy His loving presence. Be sure to meditate on all of the things you've been considering in this session.

CRAZY LOVE

PROFILE OF THE LUKEWARM

For more information on the material in this session, read chapter 4 of the book *Crazy Love: Overwhelmed by a Relentless God*.

The thought of sitting down and examining myself is terrifying. In all honesty, I know there is sin in my life. I know there are areas of my life that I don't want to submit to God. It's not particularly fun to open up my life for scrutiny.

Yet this is exactly what Paul tells us to do: "Examine yourselves, to see whether you are in the faith. Test yourselves" (2 Cor. 13:5). As frightening as that is, not examining yourself has to be even more terrifying. What if you are not the person you think you are? What if you say you love God, but you actually don't? What if you assume that you're doing fine, but the opposite is true?

Most likely, this will be the most uncomfortable session. I'm going to ask you to use this session as a self-examination. At the end of the day, you don't really need me or anyone else to tell you that you don't love God enough. For one thing, we all know that we don't love

God enough. For another thing, the most effective way for you to get to the heart of this is to be brutally honest with yourself. Another person can look at your actions and guess at your motives, but you know what drives you to do the things you do and what keeps you from doing the things you don't do.

Start by simply trying to describe yourself. With just a brief evaluation of your life, would you characterize yourself as passionate or lukewarm? Life doesn't usually fit on either end of a continuum like that, but sometimes it's helpful to look at the extremes. In this case, it's important to make stark distinctions, because Jesus' call is for us to let go of everything and follow Him. It's a call to radical discipleship. Start your self-examination by answering the question below:

1. **Would you describe yourself as totally in love with Jesus Christ? Or do the words *half-hearted, lukewarm,* and *partially committed* fit better? What evidence is there to support your answer?**

I'm struck by the two parables Jesus tells in Matthew 13:44–46. Both are incredibly short yet incredibly profound. In the first parable, a man sells everything he has to buy a treasure. In the second, a man sells everything he has to buy a pearl of great value. In these stories, we are taught to pursue the kingdom of heaven with everything we have. God and His kingdom are worth more than anything we can possibly imagine or cling to. Giving up everything we love should be a joyful prospect in light of the incomparable greatness of what we find in God Himself. These parables are easy enough to understand, but do they accurately describe your pursuit of God and His kingdom? Take a minute to read this short passage, then answer the questions below.

2. **Have you ever experienced a desire for God so intense that it would lead you to let go of everything you wanted for His sake? If so, describe that desire and explain why God is worth giving up everything for.**

3. **If you've never experienced this type of desire (or if this desire is rare in your life), which desires would you say are stronger than your desire for the Lord? Why do you think this is?**

As uncomfortable as it may be to ask yourself the preceding questions, I think this section will get even more unsettling. Below I've listed a number of Bible references from chapter 4 of *Crazy Love*. Each of these passages either describes some aspect of a lukewarm person or gives a picture of what it really means to follow Jesus. I encourage you to read through each passage thoughtfully and introspectively (you may also find it helpful to pick up *Crazy Love* and read the descriptions of lukewarm people that accompany these verses). Allow these descriptions to challenge your values, dreams, and actions.

4. **As you work your way through the following list, write down any thoughts that challenge you or realizations of things you need to work on.**

    Isaiah 29:13

Isaiah 58:6–7

Matthew 5:43–47

Matthew 7:21–23

Matthew 10:32–33

Matthew 21:28–31

Matthew 22:37–38

Matthew 23:5–7

Matthew 23:25–28

James 4:17

Revelation 3:1

If you have the *Crazy Love DVD Study Resource,* watch the video for session 4 now, particularly if you are meeting with a group. After the video, work through the rest of this session.

5. Based on the Scripture you've read in this session, what stands out to you the most? What hits you the hardest? Why?

6. Based on the Scripture and material you've covered in this session, what changes do you need to make in your life?

Luke 9:57–62

Luke 12:16–21

Luke 14:12–14

Luke 14:31–33

Luke 21:1–4

Romans 6:1–2

1 Timothy 6:17–18

James 1:22

Before you go any further, take a minute to consider your answers thus far. Whenever we talk about giving more of ourselves to God or living up to His standards, there is a real danger that we will respond out of guilt and fear rather than love. Both guilt and fear are strong motivators, but they give the wrong kind of motivation. The only cure for lukewarmness is love (we'll deal with this concept in greater depth in session 6).

7. **Did you answer the previous questions out of guilt and fear or out of love for God? How might more increased love for God change the way you answer the preceding questions?**

It's one thing to feel conviction about not living up to God's standard. But it's quite another to desire God so intensely that you take whatever steps are necessary to get back to pursuing Him with every ounce of your being. It's very important that our pursuit of God is not motivated by a desire to be "good enough," but by love for God and a desire to please Him with our lives.

No doubt there are many aspects of your life that need to change. But keep in mind that these changes need to flow from a heart that values God more than anything else (remember the two parables from Matt. 13:44–46). Lukewarmness is not the inevitable result of being imperfect. We're all imperfect. Lukewarmness is the inevitable result of lack of love for God. The solution is not to push yourself into behaving perfectly; the solution is to cultivate your love for God.

In the previous session, we examined God's unrelenting love for us. The only proper response to God's love is to love Him in return: "We love because he first loved us" (1 John 4:19). Remember that the most important commandment is to love God with everything we have. From this love for God flows the passion and obedience that marks our lives as followers of Jesus.

8. **What barriers can you identify in your life that keep you from loving God as you ought?**

How can you overcome these barriers?

9. Keeping in mind everything you've thought through during this session, what things can you do to cultivate a stronger love for God?

10. Spend some time in prayer. It's impossible for you to overcome your tendencies toward lukewarmness by simply trying harder. You absolutely need God's power and God's Spirit to help you overcome your lack of love for God. Ask Him to work in your heart to increase your desire for Him. Spend some time simply enjoying His presence and seeking to draw near to Him. If it's been a while since you've felt close to God, be honest about that and ask God to restore your intimacy and fellowship with Him.

PROFILE OF THE LUKEWARM

SERVING LEFTOVERS TO A HOLY GOD

For more information on the material in this session, read chapter 5 of the book *Crazy Love: Overwhelmed by a Relentless God.*

You can tell a lot about what type of person you are by looking at the way you respond to God. Examining your church attendance record, the amount you give to charitable organizations, or the number of Christian books you've read will tell you some things. But these (and a number of other superficial qualifications for being a "good Christian") are merely externals. If you were to strip away all of your activities and associations, what would be left? At the core of your being, what do you think about God? How do you respond to Him?

Jesus told the parable of the sower to illustrate the point that different types of people respond to God in different ways. In session 3 we examined God's overwhelming, relentless love for us. The only possible response to this type of love is to give ourselves wholly to God in loving surrender. Right? Sadly, we all know that this isn't the case. In the parable of the sower, some do respond to the seed of God's Word in loving obedience. But some hear and reject

God's truth. Others seem to be growing and following for a while, but as soon as things get difficult they give up. Still others follow joyfully at first, then get caught up in the cares of the world and the pull of possessions and choose a different course.

The parable of the sower provides a perfect opportunity for us to pause and answer the question: How do I respond to God? Which type of soil am I? Take a minute to read this parable in Luke 8:4–15. Try to appreciate the force of Jesus' words. Read it honestly, trying to see where you fit in the parable. Then answer the question below.

1. **After reading the parable of the soils and Jesus' explanation of it, which type of soil do you think best describes you? Why?**

I think that most people would like to believe that God doesn't expect too much from us. I'd say that most Christians live as though God wants a minimal commitment from us but is absolutely thrilled when we surprise Him by going above and beyond. As comforting as that may be, I simply don't find any hint of this in Scripture.

What I see instead is God warning us again and again about the dangers of being lukewarm. He warns us against thinking we're committed when we're really not. He calls us to let go of everything we have and follow Him. The harshest words in the Bible are reserved for those who maintain a minimal external commitment to the Lord but don't pursue Him passionately (the best known examples of this are Jesus' harsh rebukes of the Pharisees).

One of the most terrifying passages in Scriptures is found in the opening chapter of Malachi. At the time when Malachi was prophesying, the people of Israel were going through the religious motions. They were frequenting the temple, offering sacrifices, and saying prayers. I can't imagine that their level of religious commitment was any lower than what you would find in most American churches. But in the book of Malachi, God takes the notion that half-hearted worship is better than no worship at all and blows it completely out of the water.

Take a few minutes to read Malachi 1:6–14. As you read it, try to picture the religious scene. What were God's people doing in this passage? How might their actions look in a typical American church? And make sure you pay attention to the way God responds.

2. **According to Malachi 1, what were the Israelites doing wrong in their approach to God? Why was this such a big deal?**

3. **In this passage, how does God respond to their half-hearted sacrifices?**

4. **We no longer offer animal sacrifices, but we would be foolish to disregard this warning. In what ways do you think we may be in danger of making the same mistakes that the Israelites made in Malachi 1?**

The book of Malachi stands as a shocking wake-up call to those of us who believe that something is better than nothing when it comes to following Jesus. Think about it for a minute: Do we really expect God to be thrilled when we look at His incredible gift of love and casually reply, "I guess that's worth minimal commitment on my part"? There's no way!

It should be enough for us that God is the holy creator of the entire universe. But when we add the fact that this God also loves us unconditionally and laid down His life so that His rebellious creation could enjoy eternal fellowship with Him, our mediocre response to God not only looks ridiculous, it looks like pure evil. And that's exactly what God calls the Israelite's half-hearted worship in Malachi: It's not too bad, non-ideal, or better than nothing—it's evil!

I'm going to ask you to pause again and think about your response to God. Would you say that you're absolutely committed to Him? Or would you say that you spend your best time and energy on yourself, then give Him whatever is left at the end of the day? The way you answer this question is essential for deciding where you go from here. After hearing a warning like Malachi 1, there's no more pretending that everything is just fine. It's time to honestly evaluate yourself and decide what it's going to take to pursue God as though nothing else matters.

5. Would you say that you are guilty of serving "leftovers" to God? How so, or why not?

Jesus is not at all ambiguous about what He calls us to—we just have a difficult time accepting it. He says very simply, "If anyone would come after me, let him deny himself and take up his cross and follow me. For whoever would save his life will lose it, but whoever loses his life for my sake will find it" (Matt. 16:24–25).

For a significant portion of my life, my tendency would be to read a passage like this and then think through the reasons why Jesus couldn't be saying what He seemed to be saying.

I'm learning to fight that tendency and let Jesus speak for Himself. If you were to let go of everything you'd like Jesus to say to you and take His words at face value, how should these words affect your life? The answer may be fairly simple, but allow yourself to think through the implications of Jesus' statement and the impact it should have on your life.

6.   **What does it mean to take up your cross and follow Jesus? What do you think Matthew thought those words meant when he wrote them down?**

7.   **Being as practical as possible, describe some of the ways that taking up your cross and following Jesus might play out in your unique setting.**

It's impossible to talk about some of Jesus' more difficult commands without someone accusing you of preaching perfectionism. I flatly reject the notion that God only accepts perfect people. This is the opposite of the gospel. But this accusation is something of a red herring that could lead us away from taking Jesus' words seriously. The fact of the matter is that Jesus calls us to let go of everything and follow Him.

The incredible reality of God's love should cause us to respond with an intense and all-consuming love for God. If we were perfect, we would need no salvation. But precisely because we are imperfect, sinful, weak human beings, God intervenes in His infinite grace and grants us the unbelievable privilege of pursuing Him with every ounce of our being. It's not about us being perfect in ourselves; it's about adopting a posture of obedience where we let go of everything we have and joyfully cling to God. Though we will fail, our passion, love, and commitment to God are never in question.

8. **How would you explain the difference between living a perfect life and developing a posture of obedience to God? Why is the distinction important?**

If you have the *Crazy Love DVD Study Resource,* watch the video for session 5 now, particularly if you are meeting with a group. After the video, work through the rest of this session.

I know the material in this session is hard-hitting. Believe it or not, I don't like to be harsh just for the sake of being harsh. All I'm trying to do is point out that there is an all-powerful, holy God who rules this universe, that He loves us more than we could possibly imagine, and that He calls us to pursue Him in a loving and obedient relationship.

I know it's uncomfortable to question your motives and commitment. But I'm simply pointing out that God isn't calling us to a lukewarm Christian life. In fact, God hates the lukewarm Christian life. Because of this frightening reality, I'm going to ask you to be honest about your doubts. I don't want you to question God or His love for you, but I do want you to question some of the assumptions you've held. I want you to ask which type of soil you are, what kind of worshipper you are, and whether you really love God more than anything in the world. This time of self-examination could be the most important of your life.

9. As you think back over the material you've covered for this session, do you have any doubts about your salvation or your relationship with God? Be very honest here. Where did this session leave you?

10. Whether or not you've decided that you're living the "lukewarm life" at this point in your life, write down some thoughts about the solution to lukewarmness (if you don't need this right now, you will at some point). How do you overcome apathy and increase your love for God?

11. End this session by spending some time with God. As you do, meditate on the following questions. Don't answer quickly; just consider these things in God's presence, and do whatever business with God is necessary: Am I willing to say to God that He can have whatever He wants? Do I believe that wholehearted commitment to Him is more important than any other thing or person in my life? Do I believe that nothing I do in this life will ever matter unless it is about loving God and loving the people He has made?

SERVING LEFTOVERS TO A HOLY GOD

WHEN YOU'RE IN LOVE

For more information on the material in this session, read chapter 6 of the book *Crazy Love: Overwhelmed by a Relentless God*.

Love changes everything. It does more than make us feel happy in the midst of difficult situations. Love actually changes our approach to God. God's love for us means that we are called into a close relationship with our Creator. Our love for God means that following Him is not a tedious duty but a joyful privilege.

We have a strong tendency to want to be good enough for God. Even though we know God loves us unconditionally and accepts us solely by grace, it's so easy for us to slip back into a merit-based relationship with God. But the gospel is all about love. God's love is not dependent on our achievements or greatness; God's love is most clearly seen in the fact that He died for us *while we were sinners* (see Romans 5:8).

As much as we value God's love for us, it would be difficult for most of us to say that our relationship with God is completely characterized by love. So many Christians can't get past the nagging feeling that they need to somehow pay God back for what He has given them. They're enslaved by the notion that they need to work harder to make up for their inadequacies. I'm sure we'd all deny this, but deep down, many of us carry this burden. Take a minute to assess whether your relationship with God is characterized by love or by a burdensome desire to impress God.

1. **Which of the following statements, if any, sound like you? Describe what that looks like in your life. Also, talk about why you tend to go down this path.**

    I feel incredibly guilty about how badly I fail at obeying God.

    Sometimes I avoid prayer because I'm sure God is frustrated with me and I don't want to deal with what it will feel like to be with Him.

    I'm scared of how mad God probably is with me.

    I try really hard to make up for my inadequacies and my imperfect obedience to God.

    I try really hard to do what God wants because I'm supposed to, but I often wish I could just do what I want for a change.

2. **What if God loves you so much that He doesn't want to see you with frustration, doesn't want you to be shackled with guilt or fear, and doesn't want you driven to try harder? How does it affect you to think of Him like that?**

Whenever love and freedom are emphasized, there are always people who grow suspicious. After all, the Bible has a lot to say about commandments, good works, and moral living. But the emphasis on love is not an attempt to get away from obeying God or following Jesus. Love actually drives us to do those things.

The Bible emphasizes love, not as a replacement for the law of God, but as the fulfillment of it. In Galatians 5:13–14 Paul says, "For you were called to freedom, brothers. Only do not use your freedom as an opportunity for the flesh, but through love serve one another. For the whole law is fulfilled in one word: 'You shall love your neighbor as yourself.'" Incredibly, rather than leading us to serve our own passions and desires, love actually leads us back to serving others and fulfilling God's commands.

3. **Think about Paul's words in Galatians 5:13–14. How do love and freedom keep us away from sin?**

Not only should an increasing love for God lead us to obey Him and serve the people around us, but it should also change the way we do these things. In the same way that a person in love will happily drive for hours to be with the one he loves, so our love for God leads us to delight in doing the things that God wants us to do. Every religion in the world involves some form of appeasing a higher power, but the heart of Christianity is a loving relationship with God. It's not about achievement; it's about fellowship. It's not about obligation; it's about love.

4.   **Consider the difference between serving God out of love versus obligation. How does obedience to God change as our love for God grows?**

Now take some time to consider your own relationship with God. It's one thing to praise the value of serving God out of love rather than obligation, but it's another thing to incorporate those changes into your daily routine and fundamental posture toward God. It's easy to talk about these things in an abstract sense, but it's incredibly important to try on these concepts and see what they should actually look like in the context of your everyday life.

So consider your experience with the Christian life. How would you describe it? Do you experience the freedom that Paul talks about in Galatians? Or do you feel enslaved by a bunch of rules? Avoid any tendency to give the "right" answers to these questions. Try to honestly evaluate your relationship with God and your approach to the Christian life.

5.   **Does the Christian life feel free to you? Or do you feel bound to obey a system of moral commands? Be descriptive in your answer.**

If you have the *Crazy Love DVD Study Resource,* watch the video for session 6 now, particularly if you are meeting with a group. After the video, work through the rest of this session.

Different people tend to respond to God in different ways. Whether it's your background, your relationships, your disposition, your theology, or something else, you have a somewhat unique way of relating to God. To some extent, that's healthy. God made you to be who you are, and your relationship with Him should reflect that.

But there's another sense in which your unique situation presents you with unique obstacles to overcome. Some people have no trouble approaching God with reverence but can't imagine what it would be like to relate to God intimately. Others are the exact opposite. We all have some sort of baggage that colors our thoughts, feelings, and actions toward God.

Like any personal relationship, your relationship with God will probably look a little bit different from anyone else's. But it's helpful to identify and evaluate your tendencies. As you do so, think about whether your relationship with God reflects the love He has for you and the love that should characterize your relationship with Him.

6. **Which is more difficult for you, relating to God with intimacy or approaching Him with reverence? Why do you think this is more difficult for you?**

7. **What baggage do you carry around with you? How do you think this affects your relationship with God?**

8. **Does your relationship with God resemble an "in love" relationship? How so, or how not?**

As Paul evaluated the situation in Galatia, he recognized that they were missing the point. He saw a tendency among some of the Jewish Christians to center their religious life in their Jewish identity. They believed circumcision and adherence to the law were vitally important, and they taught other Christians accordingly. Paul's answer to this issue is striking, both in its power and its simplicity. He says, "For in Christ Jesus neither circumcision nor uncircumcision counts for anything, but only faith working through love" (Gal. 5:6).

Imagine if we applied this line of thinking to our lives. What if you could truly sum up your life by saying, "The only thing that matters is faith working itself out through love"? I believe in love, and I can honestly say that I love God passionately. But there are many times when my life does not reflect the fact that faith working through love is all that matters. Take a minute to examine your lifestyle in light of Paul's words.

9. **As you look at the way you interact with the people around you (both inside and outside the church), would you say those interactions are best characterized by love? Why do you say that?**

Another testament to the power of love in our relationships with God is found throughout the psalms. It doesn't take much effort to find psalms expressing a profound love for God. I always find these psalms inspiring. They push me to go deeper in my relationship with God. They tell me that there's still further to go—that there's still more fellowship and intimacy with God to be had.

10. **Take some time to meditate on the following psalms. Try to put yourself in the psalmists' shoes and feel the emotions they felt. How do these psalms compare to your relationship with God? Do you relate to them at all? Make some notes below. And if you find a gap between what the psalmist says and your own experience, consider stopping and asking, "Lord, please help me see You this way. Help me respond to You like this."**

Psalm 4:7–8

Psalm 16:11

Psalm 28:7

Psalm 90:14

Psalm 119:111

Psalm 131:2

We have covered this concept briefly in earlier sessions, but it's absolutely foundational to the Christian life: The solution to loving God more is not simply trying harder. I'm sure there will be plenty of effort involved, but ultimately, loving God requires His work in our hearts. Remember that love is one of the fruits of the Spirit. Think about what that phrase means: *fruits of the Spirit.* They are the natural by-product of the Holy Spirit working in our lives, changing us from the inside out.

In light of this, it's completely appropriate (and necessary) for us to ask God for more love. We have plenty of reasons to love God, but since we are dependent on Him for every aspect of our existence, we still need to rely on Him to produce love in us. Remember 1 John 4:19: "We love because he first loved us."

11. **After going through the previous sessions, have you been asking God to increase your love for Him and for the people He has placed in your life? If so, what changes have you seen? If not, what is keeping you from doing this?**

12. **It's time to stop talking about loving God and start spending time directly with Him. Use everything you've thought through in this session as you approach God. Be honest with Him about your lack of love for Him. Tell Him about your struggles and ask Him to produce more love in your heart. (You may find the prayer on the last page of chapter 6 to be helpful in approaching God with complete honesty.)**

WHEN YOU'RE IN LOVE

YOUR BEST LIFE … LATER

For more information on the material in this session, read chapter 7 of the book *Crazy Love: Overwhelmed by a Relentless God.*

Should the reality of life after death affect our lives before death? Paul thought so. In the midst of speaking about the implications of Jesus' resurrection for our lives, Paul said, "If the dead are not raised, 'Let us eat and drink, for tomorrow we die'" (1 Cor. 15:32). This statement reflects the beliefs of the ancient Epicurean philosophers who believed that death was nothing—it's simply the separation of the elements that make up our bodies and souls. How would the Epicureans advise us to live in light of this inevitable end? Enjoy life to the fullest, because this is all we get.

Paul would agree with this philosophy of life, but only if the dead are not raised. For Paul, the reality of the resurrection and the hope of eternal life should have a profound impact on the way we live our lives now. If all we get is this life, why not live it up? But if the dead are in fact raised, then our lives should reflect that reality. We should live as though we believe in life after death. We should not be trying to find as much pleasure as possible in this life, because we believe that the best is yet to come. What we do in this life matters, and our lives should reflect our belief about where history is headed.

I don't think any Christian will seriously disagree with what I've just said. But take a minute to think about the implications of the resurrection for your life. Start by asking yourself a simple question that should have a simple answer: Do you believe in life after death? If the answer is yes, then take some time to consider whether that belief changes anything about the way you live now.

1. **Is your life shaped in any way by the hope of eternal life? If so, how? If not, why do you think this is the case?**

If we truly believe that life continues after death, we would be foolish to ignore those aspects of our existence that will continue to matter long after our life here is ended. Take some time to evaluate the things you value, the things you pursue with your time, money, and energy. Consider whether you find more fulfillment in Christ or apart from Him.

2. **Have you ever come to a point where you realized the foolishness of seeking fulfillment outside of Christ? If so, what prompted that realization and what was it like?**

Up to this point in our study, we've spent a lot of time discussing the importance of complete surrender to God. As simple as that may sound (or maybe it doesn't sound simple at all!), complete surrender to God does not come naturally. As Christians, we want to please God. But all Christians have tried pleasing God on their own terms. We want God to be pleased with us, but we imagine that we can serve Him adequately without sacrificing our comfort—this is the essence of serving our leftovers to a holy God. But Jesus calls us to pick up our cross and follow Him, and anything less amounts to disobedience.

3. **Have you ever come to a point where you realized that it's impossible to please God apart from wholehearted surrender? If so, what prompted that realization, and what was it like?**

4. **In what other ways have you tried to please God?**

Hebrews 11:6 says it's impossible to please God without faith. After this potent statement, the rest of the chapter contains a long list of faithful people and what they did for God through faith. None of the people in the list is perfect, but they all surrendered themselves to God through faith, and God used them to accomplish amazing things.

Take some time to read through Hebrews 11. Try to identify with some of the characters listed in this inspiring passage. These people were simple, sinful, weak human beings. What the author of Hebrews admires about them is their faith and how that faith played out in their lives. Think about the things that God used these people to do and how foolish these things would be if life ended with death. As you try to identify with these people, begin to analyze your life in light of these acts of faith.

5.   **Which examples of faith inspire you the most? Why?**

6.   **Have you ever done anything that wouldn't make any sense if all we have is this life, but makes perfect sense in light of eternity? If so, describe what you did and why you did it. If not, why do you think you've never done anything like this?**

In chapter 7 of *Crazy Love,* I mentioned that one of my college professors challenged me to ask myself what I was doing that requires faith. This is a convicting question to put to yourself. Most of us can explain every aspect in our lives without appealing to supernatural power or godly motivations. Take some time to consider this question yourself, especially in light of what you read in Hebrews 11.

7.   **What are you doing right now that requires faith?**

The solution to lukewarmness and the appropriate motivation for wholehearted surrender to God is love. Remember that this is the greatest commandment. But I've known a lot of people who talk a lot about loving God yet treat the people around them horribly. For these people, loving God is an abstract concept that doesn't necessarily affect the other areas of their lives.

But the Bible doesn't speak about love in such ambiguous terms. For the biblical writers, love is real and concrete. Love transforms us from the inside out; it spreads to every aspect of our existence.

Take two particularly potent examples from 1 John. Read through 1 John 3:16–20 and 4:19–21. Allow your thinking to be shaped by John's descriptions of what it means to love God. As you read these passages, evaluate your love for God in light of your love for the people God has placed in your life. After you've spent some time with these two sections of Scripture, answer the questions below thoughtfully.

8. **Describe the way you tend to interact with people. Would you characterize this as sacrificial love? Why or why not?**

9. **Think very practically here: How should your love for God flow out in sacrifice for the sake of others?**

If you have the *Crazy Love DVD Study Resource,* watch the video for session 7 now, particularly if you are meeting with a group. After the video, work through the rest of this session.

The Christian life is not about money. That is, being a Christian does not automatically mean that you should be rich. But it also doesn't automatically mean that you should be poor. There have been groups of Christians throughout history who have adamantly pursued both ends of the financial spectrum as an end in itself. Money is an important part of our daily lives, but we don't always think of our finances in light of our love for God.

Money is not the point. Love for God is the point. But this doesn't mean that we can separate our love for God from the way we pursue, gain, and spend our money. John says this explicitly in the passage you just looked at: "If anyone has the world's goods and sees his brother in need, yet closes his heart against him, how does God's love abide in him?" (1 John 3:17). The things we pursue and the way we spend our money absolutely reflect what's going on inside our hearts. Jesus gave an important warning: "Where your treasure is, there your heart will be also" (Matt. 6:21).

The easiest way to "Christianize" our finances is to declare all spending of money on non-spiritual things sinful. But this misses the point. It's about our hearts. It's about the way our love for God flows in the way we care for and bless other people. It's about enjoying God's good gifts so much that we go to great lengths to enable other people to enjoy them as well. Ultimately, allowing God to control our hearts will also mean allowing Him to control our wallets.

Using our money to bless other people is not the only way to express our love for God, but it is an important way that we often sidestep for the sake of our own comfort.

10. Assess your earning, saving, and spending habits in terms of wholehearted devotion to God. Which of these habits might be foolish in light of eternity? How so?

11. Do you have any possessions or resources that God might be calling you to give away to someone who is in need? What and why?

12. End this session by praying that God would work in your heart. The concept of wholehearted devotion to God can quickly degenerate into a legalistic denial of all God's gifts. Instead, ask God to show you distractions in your life and expose things that you desire more than you desire God. Ask Him to decrease your desire for these things and increase your desire for Him. Ask Him to multiply your love for Him to such an extent that it spills out into every area of your life and into the lives of the people He has placed in your life.

YOUR BEST LIFE ... LATER

PROFILE OF THE OBSESSED

For more information on the material in this session, read chapter 8 of the book *Crazy Love: Overwhelmed by a Relentless God*.

We've all known people who are obsessed with different things. I've known people who are obsessed with cars, good food, music, Disney—all sorts of things. We characterize these people as obsessed because they think and talk about these things all the time. Their obsession dictates their lifestyle. It defines them. They don't seem to recognize that other people aren't interested in their obsession; they just keep talking about their favorite music (or whatever) until you can think up a good enough excuse to step away.

Obsession is the opposite of lukewarmness. So another way of saying that we should stop being lukewarm is saying that we should become obsessed. But what does obsession with Jesus look like? Does it mean that we fill our homes with trinkets from the local Christian bookstore? Does it mean filling your wardrobe with Christian T-shirts or your iPod with Christian music?

It may end up looking a little different for each person, but if you're obsessed with Jesus, you'll be defined by your obsession. You won't be able to stop thinking about Him or talking about Him. More importantly, you'll constantly find yourself acting like Him. If you're obsessed with Jesus, you'll start looking a lot like Him. You'll go the places Jesus would go and do the things He did, no matter what sacrifice or discomfort it brings.

Most Christians are not obsessed with Jesus. There are big parts of their lives that are devoted to God and His will, but for most Christians, there's a line they'll rarely (if ever) cross. That line is usually personal comfort and safety. Sure, we'll all put money in the offering, but we would never forego our dreams in order to give more. We'll help people who are in need, but only for a while, only until it begins to infringe on our lifestyle. We'll do crazy things for God, but not if it's dangerous.

As a church, we used to travel to Mexico every year and assist local churches in their ministries. Every year, hundreds of us would cross the border and sacrifice our time, money, and comfort in order to help people in need. But then Mexico got more dangerous. The news media began to report on murders and abductions. We began to hear rumors that it wasn't safe to minister in Mexico any longer. And guess what? A lot of people stopped going to Mexico with us.

I'm not suggesting that these people are cowards or that they don't love God. But I think it shows that there are some things we'll do for God as long as it doesn't threaten our safety or comfort. We may as well pray, "God, please use me however You want, send me wherever You want to do whatever You want. Unless it's dangerous. Then don't send me." This is not the prayer of an obsessed person. When you're obsessed with Jesus, you love and trust Him so much that you pray without qualification: "God, use me in whatever way You think is best. Period."

1. **Would you say that you place personal comfort and safety above what God may want to do in you and through you? How so?**

Risk is a tricky concept. On the one hand, we use "risk" to describe actions that are just plain stupid—like speeding on a motorcycle without a helmet or gambling to pay off a debt. But risk isn't always stupid. Following the directions of a loving God who has never led anyone astray ever is not stupid.

Obeying God will not always lead us where we want to go—throughout history many have lost their freedom, possessions, families, and even their lives by obediently following God. But since God is the ruler of this world, since He is the one who works ultimate justice and gives ultimate rewards, then any risk or sacrifice that comes through following Him is not stupid.

Think about your lifestyle and pursuits. Can you say that your life is characterized by a devotion to God that would follow Him anywhere at any time? Or might you be better known for playing it safe and pursuing your plans in your way? I'm not trying to convince you to go out and do the ten riskiest things you can think of. But most of us have a pretty good idea of some risks that God wants us to take. Think through what some of those things might be and what steps you'd need to take to make those things happen.

2.   What risks might God be calling you to take?

Sadly, today's church is not a breeding ground for those obsessed with Jesus. You would think that the church would promote that type of obsession, that anyone who has been a Christian for any length of time would be growing in their passion and encouraged to get out there and do whatever God may be calling them to do.

But that scenario isn't typical. Instead, most people who are developing an obsession with Jesus will joyfully tell another Christian about their growing passion and the risks they're planning to take for God's sake. Then their fellow Christians will respond by pointing out the dangers involved and suggesting a safer, more comfortable course of action.

Maybe you've been on one side or the other in that scenario. Most Christians have been. If you have, try to assess that situation. If you were to relive that situation now, how would you react? What would you do differently? Or to put it another way, how would an obsessed person act in that sort of situation (whether it's pursuing some risky course of action or counseling someone else who is considering it)? Take the time to think it through now so you can better work together with the other Christians in your life to accomplish everything God calls you to do.

3. **Have you ever tried to do something risky or crazy for God, only to be discouraged from doing so by another Christian? Have you ever been that person who tries to discourage other Christians from doing crazy or risky things for God? Describe your experience and how you think God would want you to respond in those situations.**

One common danger among people who do crazy things for God is the desire to be recognized for what you're doing. It's not that all recognition is always bad, but we can do good things in such a way that it makes us look good. I can preach a really convicting sermon about the need to glorify God, yet do so in a way that puts my preaching skills on display. If I'm not careful, this motivation very subtly nestles in beside some better motivations for serving God, and it may even overtake them.

Think through your unique situation in light of this. What acts of service do you do for God, or what things might He be calling you to do? There is a way to do each of these things that draws the attention to you and a way that draws the attention to God. Think about how you can point all of the attention to God.

4. **What would it look like to do incredible things for God, but in a way where God gets all the glory and attention, rather than you?**

Obsession leads people to ignore all sorts of social norms. Obsession with Jesus is no different. Read through Luke 14:12–14. In the context, Jesus is speaking to a number of guests at a dinner party. Being invited into someone's home and fed a meal is always a great honor. It's a blessing for those people who get to enjoy the food and company. As Jesus sat among the other guests at the dinner party, He turned to the host and told him about the type of people He would have invited.

We all want to spend time with people who are just like us. We enjoy blessing the people we like. But Jesus' guest list looks much different. And if we are truly obsessed with Jesus—thinking the way He thinks, doing the things He does, feeling the things He feels—then this should begin to shape our experience. Read through this passage reflectively and ask yourself how Jesus' words should apply in your setting.

5. **Are there people in your life who might fit Jesus' description in Luke 14:12–14? If so, who are they, and what needs do they have?**

6. **What blessings has God given you that you can use to bless these people? How can you go about doing this?**

In light of what we've looked at thus far, would you say that you're obsessed with Jesus? In session 4, I asked you to analyze your life in light of some biblical descriptions of a lukewarm person. Now I'm going to ask you to analyze your life in terms of an obsessed person. This will probably be very convicting.

Remember that the goal is not attaining perfection by trying harder. Read through this list and make some notes about how your life does or doesn't match the profile of the obsessed. As you find areas that need to be addressed (we will all find plenty of things to work on), you'll be identifying things you can bring before God and the other Christians in your life. You should be asking God to work in your heart and asking your group to support you in pursuing God wholeheartedly.

7. **Read through the following statements about people who are obsessed with Jesus. Which do you find most challenging? Make some notes about why these challenge you and how you may need to adjust your lifestyle.**

People who are obsessed with Jesus give freely and openly, without censure. Obsessed people love those who hate them and who can never love them back.

People who are obsessed with Jesus aren't consumed with their personal safety and comfort above all else. Obsessed people care more about God's kingdom coming to this earth than their lives being shielded from pain or distress.

People who are obsessed with Jesus live lives that connect them with the poor in some way or another. Obsessed people believe that Jesus talked about money and the poor so often because it was really important to Him.

Obsessed people are more concerned with obeying God than doing what is expected or fulfilling the status quo. A person who is obsessed with Jesus will do things that don't always make sense in terms of success or wealth on this earth.

A person who is obsessed with Jesus knows that the sin of pride is always a battle. Obsessed people know that you can never be "humble enough," and so they seek to make themselves less known and Christ more known.

People who are obsessed with Jesus do not consider service a burden. Obsessed people take joy in loving God by loving His people.

People who are obsessed with God are known as givers, not takers. Obsessed people genuinely think that others matter as much as they do, and they are particularly aware of those who are poor around the world.

A person who is obsessed thinks about heaven frequently. Obsessed people orient their lives around eternity; they are not fixed only on what is here in front of them.

A person who is obsessed is characterized by committed, settled, passionate love for God, above and before every other thing and every other being.

People who are obsessed are raw with God; they do not attempt to mask the ugliness of their sins or their failures. Obsessed people don't put it on for God; He is their safe place, where they can be at peace.

People who are obsessed with God have an intimate relationship with Him. They are nourished by God's Word throughout the day because they know that forty minutes on Sunday is not enough to sustain them for a whole week, especially when they will encounter so many distractions and alternative messages.

A person who is obsessed with Jesus is more concerned with his or her character than comfort. Obsessed people know that true joy doesn't depend on circumstances or environment; it is a gift that must be chosen and cultivated, a gift that ultimately comes from God.

A person who is obsessed with Jesus knows that the best thing he can do is be faithful to his Savior in every aspect of his life, continually saying, "Thank You!" to God. An obsessed person knows there can never be intimacy if he is always trying to pay God back or work hard enough to be worthy. He revels in his role as a child and friend of God.

If you have the *Crazy Love DVD Study Resource*, watch the video for session 8 now, particularly if you are meeting with a group. After the video, work through the rest of this session.

Even though I believe the American church tends to be characterized more by lukewarmness than by obsession, we still have many incredible examples of what an obsessed church would look like. You may have plenty of obsessed people in your church—people who love Jesus like crazy and push you to do the same. But even if you're not aware of any contemporary examples, you don't have to look any further than the book of Acts.

Acts describes a church that is absolutely obsessed with Jesus Christ. On every page we find examples of people believing, saying, giving, and doing everything that Jesus calls them to.

But sometimes reading Acts leaves me a bit discouraged because it doesn't match the churches I see around me. I sometimes wonder if we've given up on this vision completely. I wonder if our churches are ready to simply shrug their shoulders and write off the early church as a nice dream but a practical impossibility. My prayer is that our churches would be increasingly filled with dreamers who look back to the early church and long to be characterized by the same type of obsession.

8. **Describe what your gathering of Christians would look like if you began to live the type of obsessed Christian life that characterized the early church. Try to be both practical (be specific) and imaginative (think outside the box).**

9. **How can you join together with and commit to the other Christians in your life so that you can help one another live this type of devoted life?**

10. You've been thinking through some pretty audacious concepts in this session. Spend some time praying that God would move this beyond wishful thinking. Passion, obsession, and love can only come from God. Pray that He would work in your heart and in the other Christians around you to create a community that is characterized by obsession with Jesus. Ask Him to do amazing things through you in such a way that He receives all of the glory.

PROFILE OF THE OBSESSED

WHO REALLY LIVES THAT WAY?

For more information on the material in this session, read chapter 9 of the book *Crazy Love: Overwhelmed by a Relentless God.*

If you have the *Crazy Love DVD Study Resource*, watch the video for session 9 now, particularly if you are meeting with a group. After the video, work through the rest of this session.

At this point, you may have the feeling that devoting yourself wholeheartedly to God is a noble goal but that it's unrealistic and you'll never reach that point. I understand this concern. I have never reached a point where I felt as though I had reached my goal. As the Holy Spirit works in us, we will always be growing—and we will always have further to go. Paul said, "Not that I have already obtained this or am already perfect, but I press on" (Phil. 3:12).

That's the key: pressing on. But we have a tendency to get discouraged and give up. I am always so thankful for the compelling examples that God has placed in my life. Looking at the faith and love of these ordinary people gives me hope that following Jesus is possible, that God does use imperfect people to do extraordinary things.

I also love the fact that these people have developed a reputation for being devoted to God. It makes me want to be an example to the people in my life—even leaving a legacy, putting my faith into practice so that I can inspire others to pursue God with everything they have.

1. **Who has God put in your life who serves as a good example of what it means to follow Jesus? (You can also refer to some of the examples listed in chapter 9 of *Crazy Love*.) Why do you admire these people?**

2. **What character qualities, activities, and attitudes do these people possess that you would like to imitate in your own life? What would it take to make that a reality?**

3. **What legacy do you want to leave behind? What do you want to be known for?**

Whenever I think about a life characterized by boldly following God wherever He leads, I always think about Elijah. When I read about Elijah in the Old Testament, he seems to show up in some pretty random places with some pretty important messages from God. When God calls him to do something that seems crazy, Elijah just does it. I don't know exactly what that would look like in our modern world, but I can't help but want to imitate Elijah's faith.

When I think about the incredible things Elijah was able to do, I feel disconnected. How can I relate to someone who raises the dead and calls fire down from heaven? And yet James makes an incredible statement about Elijah: "Elijah was a man with a nature like ours" (James 5:17). He was just an ordinary guy. So I can relate to him. If God could do it through Elijah, He can do it through me; He can do it through you. Take a minute to read James 5:13–18 and then answer the questions below.

4. Why does James refer to Elijah in this passage? What point is he making?

5. How should James' reference to Elijah shape your approach to the Christian life?

In the opening section of his letter to the Colossians, Paul prays that they will be filled with the knowledge of God's will. That statement terrifies me. Have you ever honestly asked yourself whether you want to know God's will for your life? I know we say we want to know God's will, but what if you knew with precision everything God wanted you to do, everything He wanted you to say, everywhere He wanted you to go, and everything He wanted you to give up? My fleshly side would rather be ignorant—at least then I could explain to God that I didn't know He wanted me to do those things.

I think we encounter a similar problem when we talk about a wholehearted devotion to God. I'm quick to affirm that I want to let go of my comfort and follow God's leading. But when it really comes down to it, the thought scares me. What if He takes me somewhere I don't want to go? What if He asks for something I don't want to let go of? I think honesty requires most of us to admit a similar fear about following God completely.

6. **Do you have any fears about what it would mean if you truly followed God's leading regardless of where He might take you? If so, take a minute to articulate those fears.**

7. **What do you think God would say to those fears? (If you can think of any Scripture that applies here, write them down.)**

8. **Describe one or two tangible steps that could help you overcome these fears.**

9. **What other people has God placed in your life who may be able to partner with you in this? How might they be able to help? If you can't think of anybody, how can you find some people like this?**

As inspired as you may be by this point to let go of everything and simply follow Jesus, it's incredibly easy for most of us to get derailed. For most people, all it takes is one excuse to fall back into the same comfortable, lukewarm lifestyle they're used to. Perhaps you've started down this road in the past, but you stopped for some reason.

If that's the case, it will be helpful for you to consider some of the excuses you've used in the past. When your passion for following Jesus begins to fade, how do you rationalize your return to lukewarmness? Do you say you're too busy at this stage in your life? Do you promise yourself that you'll follow Jesus later? Do you blame the other Christians around you for not being on board? Maybe you tell yourself you can't follow Jesus fully until your church has better worship or more convicting preaching.

I'm not suggesting that we ignore our imperfections. Without a doubt, we're all going to fail as we seek to follow Jesus completely. But in order to move forward we need to identify and discredit the excuses we appeal to. Take a minute to examine some of the excuses that have derailed you in the past.

10. **What excuses have you used in the past? Why and how should you move beyond these excuses?**

One of the most common excuses for not taking action is the well-intentioned statement, "This isn't the right time to make major changes to my lifestyle. I'll start soon." How many people have gone for years—even decades—still clinging to this delusion?

If Jesus is worth following at all, then He is worth following now! If God really is as great as the Bible says He is, then every other pursuit and every single excuse pales in comparison. How could we possibly choose anything over God? Think back to Jesus' parable in Matthew 13:44: "The kingdom of heaven is like treasure hidden in a field, which a man found and covered up. Then in his joy he goes and sells all that he has and buys that field." There is no guilt or obligation here. The man in the parable simply realizes that what he has found is absolutely incomparable and acts out of joy.

If you really love God with this intensity—if you even *want* to love God like this—then it's time to take some steps in that direction (if you haven't started already). You may not be convinced beyond any doubt of exactly what God is calling you to do, but we all know at least a few things that God would have us do in the midst of our unique setting. Think about what these things might be and start taking some steps to put your love for God into action.

11. **Rather than waiting until you finish the last session of this study, what changes to your emotions, thought processes, and lifestyle can you begin to implement right now? Also note any progress that you've made based on convictions from earlier sessions.**

12. **Close this session in prayer. Now that you're so close to the end of this study, ask God to begin cementing your resolve and moving you down the path that you need to take. Ask that He would continue to increase your love for Him. Ask Him to make your life overflow with that love. Ask Him to help you overcome all of the obstacles and excuses you will encounter.**

WHO REALLY LIVES THAT WAY?

THE CRUX OF THE MATTER

For more information on the material in this session, read chapter 10 of the book *Crazy Love: Overwhelmed by a Relentless God.*

The end is always the trickiest part of a study like this. I feel the weight of trying to get you to make the things we've studied so much a part of your life that you'll continue pursuing these things after the study is over.

But you have the trickiest role. You began this study for a reason. Most likely, you wanted to be challenged in some aspect of your lifestyle, love for God, thought process, etc. I'm confident that you didn't begin this study because you wanted to be changed for a little while and then go back to the way things were. I can tell you: Don't let that happen—make sure you put into practice everything that God has taught you through these ten sessions.

Yet we both know that what I tell you doesn't matter that much. The change you're looking for will take great honesty and resolve on your part. More than that, the change you're looking for will take great dependence on God. You'll need to continually come before God and beg Him to work in and through you. And it's that "continually" part that makes endings like this difficult. How do you move from ten neatly packaged sessions to a continual pattern of life that shapes every aspect of who you are?

All I can do is challenge you to take this session to heart. I'll be asking you to evaluate where you've come thus far and to think through steps that will take you beyond this study. If all you give are easy answers, you're not likely to follow through. Use these questions to assess your heart. Process these things in the presence of God. Ask Him to guide you into thinking, feeling, and doing everything He wants.

Start by assessing how you've changed:

1. **Looking back over what you've thought through thus far, how would you say your thoughts, emotions, and actions have been changed?**

2. **If you have experienced positive changes—greater obedience to God and deeper intimacy with Jesus—describe what it has been like to see those changes in your life. (Has it been joyful, difficult, hopeful, scary, etc.?)**

In the previous session, we examined obstacles and excuses that would keep you from living this out. This isn't exactly an obstacle, but sometimes we can read a book, hear a sermon, or go through a study and have an experience that's almost *too good*. Not that it's bad to have a powerful experience, but sometimes we get so excited that we can't figure out how to follow up the experience with action.

For a while, we can live off of the excitement. But it always fades. Unless we learn to channel that excitement into concrete habits and pursuits we can maintain in the monotony of everyday life, the experience becomes a vague memory that we'd love to recover but can't. If you've ever had an experience that eventually faded into nothing, think about what it was like and what went wrong.

3. **Have you ever had a "mountaintop experience" that faded or made a radical commitment that you failed to follow through on? What stopped you?**

One of the most dangerous enemies of passion is individualism. It doesn't matter how strong an experience you have or how passionate you become, if you're left to yourself, you're eventually going to burn out or lose interest. I don't think we have a clue how important the church is. God designed the church as a place where Christians serve, pray, live, and worship together for a reason. We can't pursue God's will in our own way. We need to take the church seriously and look to one another for help, support, and inspiration as we seek to be transformed and to transform the world around us for the glory of God.

4. **How can you partner with the Christians around you to keep this from being just another Bible study or mountaintop experience? Don't allow your answer to be vague. Practically, what would it look like to work together with other people toward this end?**

Paul highlights the significance of the church in 1 Corinthians 12:4–14. He describes the church as a body. It's incredibly diverse, but it's also completely unified because every individual part of the body is transformed and recreated by the same Lord, and every part is empowered and energized by the same Spirit. So on the one hand, we need to pursue that unity and focus on fitting together with the other parts of the body. On the other hand, we need to assess how God has made and gifted each of us individually and play our part in serving the church and the world.

Read 1 Corinthians 12:4–14. Pay attention to the metaphor Paul uses and to the connection between each person's individual gifts and the unity of the body.

5. **What unique talents, gifts, and interests do you have? What do you do passionately and well?**

6. **How might you be able to use these unique aspects of your makeup for the glory of God?**

7. **Can you think of any ways in which your unique gifts and makeup might fit well with the gifts and makeup of the other Christians around you to accomplish something much greater than you could each accomplish alone?**

In light of all of what you've written, and in light of what God may have been putting on your heart throughout this study, consider the things you should be pursuing at this point. I don't know of a specific formula for "hearing the voice of God," and I don't have any cool tricks for trying to determine His will for your life. But even though these things are very subjective, I think that most of us often have a pretty good sense of where God is leading us.

It's not always as conclusive or black and white as we'd like. It's all about pursuing God with everything we have, and in the midst of that intimacy with God, He often provides opportunities, desires, and leanings that put us in the right place at the right time. Think about how that might be happening in your life. It's not about developing a five- or ten-year plan, but consider whether God is leading you in a specific direction.

8. **What do you think God is calling you (specifically) to pursue? What nagging thoughts have stayed with you throughout this study—things you can't get out of your mind, things you keep wondering about pursuing?**

Anytime we talk about "God's will for my life," we risk focusing so much on the obscure and subjective that we miss the clear and obvious. How often do we think about when and where

God might be calling us to go, yet we neglect Jesus' simple commands? In the process of trying to find some God-given direction in life, we often forget that Jesus has given us many specific commands that we should always be following.

Jesus even says, "If you love me, you will keep my commandments" (John 14:15). So all of this talk about loving God with everything we have should lead us into a very practical and continual obedience. If we love God, we'll be doing things like loving our neighbors (Matt. 22:39), helping orphans and widows (James 1:27), pursuing humility (James 4:10), and forgiving those who do us harm (Matt. 6:14–15). Consider some of the clear commands God gives us in the Bible, and ask yourself which of these you need to begin obeying.

9. **Without waiting for a feeling or a sense of calling, what clear commands of Jesus are you neglecting that you know you need to start obeying right now?**

10. **What steps do you need to take in order to start obeying Jesus in these ways?**

Maybe you're ready to get off and running. But perhaps it would be helpful to boil this whole thing down into one point. In order to avoid confusion, try to think of the one thing that you know you ought to start doing right away. This doesn't mean you neglect all of the other things, but this could be helpful as a starting point.

11. In light of everything you've worked through in this study, what do you think is the most important change that you can commit yourself to making?

If you have the *Crazy Love DVD Study Resource,* watch the video for session 10 now, particularly if you are meeting with a group. After the video, work through the rest of this session.

12. Close your study in prayer. As we've mentioned several times throughout these ten sessions, you can't do this without God. Pray that God would empower you to follow Him into anything and everything He calls you to. Pray that God would place the right people in your life to help you through. Pray that this would not be the end of an interesting study but the beginning (or renewing) of a God-centered and Spirit-empowered lifestyle. Pray that your lifestyle and relationship with God would be characterized by the kind of love that transforms the world around you.

THE CRUX OF THE MATTER

NOTES FOR DISCUSSION LEADERS

A small group working through this material will benefit from having a discussion leader. If that's you, don't worry—you don't need to have all the answers. This workbook is discussion driven, not teacher driven. All you need is the willingness to prepare each week, guide the discussion, and rely on the Holy Spirit to work in your heart and the hearts of group members. This study can give you hands-on experience depending not on your natural leadership abilities but on the Spirit. If you pray for His help, He will give it.

DISCUSSION LEADER'S JOB DESCRIPTION

The discussion leader's job isn't to have all the answers. He or she simply needs to:

- Keep the group on track when it's tempted to go off on a tangent.
- Keep the discussion moving so that it doesn't get stuck on one question.
- Make sure that everyone gets a chance to talk and that no one dominates. (It is not necessary for every person to respond aloud to every question, but every person should have the chance to do so.)
- Make sure that the discussion remains respectful.

PREPARING FOR THE DISCUSSION

As the discussion leader, you'll probably want to read the chapters from *Crazy Love* before each session. If you can view the video ahead of time, that's great. Try to work through your own responses to the discussion questions ahead of time as well. Just before the meeting, be sure the chairs are arranged so that everyone can see one another.

GUIDING THE DISCUSSION

A few ground rules can make the discussion deeper:

- *Confidentiality:* Whatever is said in the group stays in the group. Nothing is to be repeated to those who weren't there.
- *Honesty:* We're not here to impress each other. We're here to grow and to know each other.
- *Respect:* Disagreement is welcome. Disrespect is not.

The discussion should be a conversation among the group members, not a one-on-one with the leader. You can encourage this with statements like, "Thanks, Allison. What do others of you think?" or "Does anyone have a similar experience, or a different one?"

Don't be afraid of silence—it means group members are thinking about how to answer a question. Trust that the Spirit is working in the members of your group, and wait. Sometimes it's helpful to rephrase the question in your own words. Then wait for others' responses, and avoid jumping in with your own.

I recommend discussing the numbered questions in order. Read each question aloud, and ask the group to respond. Even if an answer seems obvious, have a few people share their thoughts—you never know what will spark a challenging conversation.

If you have a copy of the *Crazy Love DVD Study Resource* (I definitely recommend this for groups), stop and watch the appropriate video when prompted. After the video, work through the remaining questions. Feel free to read a section out loud if the group is unclear on what a question is getting at. There is also a segment at the end of this section that contains explanatory notes for discussion leaders. I recommend looking these up before your group meets.

I considered including a section with answers to the questions to help you in leading the discussion. Ultimately, I decided against it, because the most profitable aspect of studying this material in a group is the discussion itself. The destination is important, but you can't get there without the journey. Where specific answers are required, I've tried to point you toward Scripture. The answer may not always jump out at you, but at the very least your discussion will be headed in the right direction.

The answers are important, but I am most concerned that people may study Jesus and never *know* Him, never be *changed* by Him. With every session, keep asking yourself and your group, "How should this change us? If we really submitted our lives to Jesus and opened ourselves up to the power of the Holy Spirit, what would He have us do, where would He have us go?" At the end of the day, it's about laying hold of the power of the Spirit in order to accomplish what God has placed us on this earth to do. It's about advancing the kingdom of God. It's about His will being done on earth as in heaven.

Most of all, spend time praying for your group. You can't talk anyone into a wholehearted devotion to God. Pray that the Spirit of God would fill your lives and do the impossible in and through you. In the book of Acts, the human actors were just ordinary, weak people, but the Holy Spirit accomplished unbelievable things through these ordinary people as they prayed and submitted themselves to following His leading. May God accomplish the extraordinary in your lives as you seek to follow Jesus with everything you've got.

SESSION 1

Question 1. Obviously, this question is purely hypothetical. Who really knows what he or she would say? But this could be a good exercise in trying to help people consider what it might be like to stand before God.

Question 2. If your group didn't read chapter 1 of *Crazy Love* before your gathering, then obviously they won't have an answer to this question. That's okay. You can either move on to the next question, or you can take a minute to assess what changes each of you think you may need to make in your lives.

Question 5. If group members have a difficult time answering this question, you can have a brainstorming session that ends with different members resolving to test out different approaches to building times of reflection into their lives. You can ask for a report on how this went at the beginning of the next session.

Questions 7–8. With these two questions, I'm wanting people to look at the pattern of their lives. If someone were to look at every aspect of your life, what would they conclude about your God? Would they think He exists for your glory, or that you exist for His?

Question 10. Revelation 4, like any section in Revelation, can be difficult to interpret. Don't worry about explaining every detail of the passage or even being certain of what the passage is trying to convey. What I'd love to see is people reading Revelation 4 and being struck by the imagery of our great and terrifying God. Ask your group which aspects of Revelation 4 hit them the hardest. You may want to have someone read the passage aloud for the group so that others can listen to it freshly.

SESSION 2

Questions 1–3. The paragraph before these questions is very important. Try not to let the discussion move on to bashing all of the good things in each other's lives. If someone mentions a good thing that they feel is a distraction, ask them to clarify *how* that thing has become a distraction. Caring for your kids may be a distraction, but it can be a ministry in itself. It might be helpful to explain that most activities are not good or bad in themselves—what makes them God-glorifying or distracting is our heart behind these things and whether we are using these things as a replacement for God.

Question 5. Basically, this question is meant to help you consider how James 4:13–17 applies to your life.

Question 8. Some group members may be tempted to focus on some of the minor details in their lives—a few minutes spent watching television here or there, the cost of their haircuts, etc. Those things may be relevant and even important, but this question will likely come down to each person's priorities. Rather than focusing on occasional activities, try to help them assess what their lives seem to be devoted to. What fills their time? Where do they spend the most money? If you find that your lives don't seem to reflect a dependence on God's grace, then talk about what changes would be necessary to put this dependence at the center of your lives.

SESSION 3

Question 1. This has become a fairly common distinction in some circles. Even if you feel like the distinction is obvious, it may still be helpful to have a few people in the group explain the difference. Sometimes we learn better by trying to articulate truths that we believe but haven't tried to explain to someone else.

Question 3. This question may be difficult. For one thing, some members of the group may be harboring a lot of bitterness toward God. In their case, the trick will be encouraging them to be honest with their feelings while still maintaining an appropriate respect and caution in speaking about God. On the other hand, you may find that your group doesn't have any questions about God's love. If this is the case, it may be helpful to ask them to share about some difficult events in their lives and then explain why these things didn't make them want to question God's love.

Question 6. It would probably be helpful to also make provisions for this. That is, once you've discussed some ways in which you can help one another, try to take some steps toward actually putting these ideas into practice.

SESSION 4

Question 4. You'll have to decide how to handle this question during the group time. You may want to ask people to share the verses that hit them the hardest, and why. Or you might pick a few that shook you personally. If you have time, you might choose to read each passage and see how it affects the members of your group.

Question 7. This isn't suggesting that group members should change their answers to the previous questions. Instead, it's trying to get at their hearts. Why did they answer the way they did? It's helpful for each person to identify whether his or her obedience is motivated more by guilt or love. It's also helpful to identify why they think this might be the case.

SESSION 5

Question 1. It may be difficult for some people to identify themselves with a type of soil from the parable. If this is the case, then consider asking them to identify with some of the circumstances in the parable (such as the cares and concerns of this world). That direct and less abstract connection might help some people to identify with the parable.

Question 2. Don't feel as though you need to be an expert on Malachi to lead a discussion on this question. Just look for the things Malachi is speaking against, such as offering imperfect sacrifices.

Question 8. This question is important because it will help people avoid a legalistic sense that every Christian should be perfected immediately simply by trying harder.

Question 9. If someone in your group admits to having some doubts about their salvation, try to help them sort through what their next step ought to be. Try to avoid giving people a false assurance by simply saying, "Oh, it's okay. I'm sure you're fine." Help them wrestle with what is causing them to doubt and how they can address those issues. Also be sure to emphasize the fact that we are saved by grace through faith (see Eph. 2:8–9). As important as it is to follow God completely, we're not saved by our own efforts. We're saved by God's grace. It's the transforming power of God's grace that produces these good works in us (Eph. 2:10). This can be a difficult issue to walk someone through. Do your best, and be sure to pray for the person. If you feel you're not able to address these concerns appropriately, consider offering to accompany your group member in meeting with your pastor.

SESSION 6

Question 1. You might want to approach this question by reading each statement and then asking, "Does anyone identify with this?" After you've gone through each statement, you might also ask if anyone has a statement of their own that they think best describes them.

Question 3. Once again, don't worry about being an expert on this passage. Simply try to identify the things that Paul says about love and freedom, and then see if you can catch his connection between these two things and avoiding sin.

Question 5. This question might warrant some follow-up questions. If someone feels bound to obey a system of moral commands, you might ask how long they've felt that way, how they developed that view, and whether they think that is the correct view or if they know it's wrong but can't help feeling that way.

Question 7. This question could raise some pretty significant issues. If so, you might want to follow a similar process to what I've outlined above in the note about session 5, question 9. Do your best to walk with that person through the issue, but if, at the end of the day, you feel like there's a lot more that needs to be addressed, consider offering to go with them to meet your pastor.

Question 10. You'll have to decide how you want to approach this question during group time. You may want to read each psalm excerpt and ask people to share their thoughts on whether they relate to these statements. But you might find it more effective to ask each person to share a passage or two that either expresses their emotions or challenges them.

SESSION 7

Question 1. This could be difficult to assess. Maybe a good way to rephrase it would be, "If you truly believed in the hope of eternal life, then how should that change the way you live right now? Do you see this reflected in your life in any way?"

Question 4. For many people, this will likely include attempts to please God through self-righteousness, rigorous rule keeping, church attendance, giving money, etc.

Question 5. It's likely that you'll encounter a few examples of faith mentioned in Hebrews 11 that you're unfamiliar with. If you want, you can find the Old Testament accounts of these people by looking up their names in a concordance, or by searching a website like www.biblegateway.com. But this probably isn't necessary. All you need to do is see what the author of Hebrews is praising about each character. Also keep in mind that in every case, the author admires these people because of their faith.

Question 7. Doing something that requires faith means you're pursuing something that doesn't seem to make sense in and of itself, but you're doing it because God commands it, and you're trusting that God will enable you to do it. Maybe it's investing in a person who seems beyond all hope. Maybe it's giving to your church or to a neighbor even though you don't have a lot of money. Ultimately, something requires faith when it requires more than merely human motivation (anyone would help someone if they were getting paid to do it, or if they knew they would receive something in return).

Question 10. Make sure this doesn't degenerate into a discussion about the ways in which everyone else wastes their money. It's easy to criticize the way other people spend their money, especially if you don't understand the heart behind it.

SESSION 8

Question 2. Make sure everyone understands that we're not advocating skydiving or drinking poison. This is about putting God's will above your desire for comfort and safety. Maybe things like feeding a homeless person, forgiving someone who harmed you, or giving a little more money than you think you should are risks that God is calling some of your group members to take.

Question 3. As you discuss this session, watch for people who become defensive. Sometimes the people who feel the most convicted are the most vocal about why God would never call someone to do this or that.

Question 7. This is a fairly long list. I recommend asking your group to share the statements that they find most helpful or challenging, and why.

Question 9. This would be a great question to follow up on. If your group begins to make plans about how they can join together in this, encourage them to follow through on this, and then bring up the subject again at your next couple of meetings. Ideally, invite someone other than you to take the responsibility for leading this effort. But if no one else is likely to lead, then you do it, but be sure to delegate as much as possible to others so that the whole group owns the initiative.

SESSION 9

Question 1. If nobody can think of any examples, you could consider reading through a couple of the examples in chapter 9 of *Crazy Love*. But it also might be a good opportunity to ask them why they don't have any examples. Maybe it's because no one in your church is very remarkable. More likely, it's because either they haven't gotten to know the people around them well enough or they tend to see the negative in people and not the positive. This shouldn't be a lecture, but it's good food for thought.

Question 3. You might have some people who make big statements, such as, "I want to lead a thousand people to the Lord." There's nothing wrong with that, but make sure people are comfortable with saying things like, "I want to be remembered as someone who loved everyone around me."

Questions 4–5. There are a couple of good answers to these questions. For one thing, James is referring to Elijah as an example of a godly man. But he's specifically referring to Elijah as an example of what faithful prayer looks like. Elijah is definitely being held up as a powerful man of God in this passage, but James' statement that Elijah was a man with a nature like ours makes Elijah a relatable role model. It gives us confidence that God can use us in a similar way.

Questions 6–7. Be sure that no one is ridiculed or even looked down on for expressing fears like this. Try to affirm that these fears are legitimate. Question 7 should launch a discussion on how those fears can and should be overcome.

Question 10. After someone shares an excuse they've used before, it might be helpful to ask, "Has anyone else used a similar excuse?"

SESSION 10

Question 1. If your group can't think of anything specific, it might be helpful even to review the titles of each session. That may help them remember what you discussed, which may help them realize ways in which they've been affected and changed.

Question 4. This would be a good time to talk about the future of your group. Should you continue meeting together? What might you choose to study next? More importantly, what activities can you pursue together, and how can you continue to pray for each other?

Questions 5–7. It would also be helpful if people point out talents they recognize in the other members of the group and suggest ways they might pursue these things to the glory of God. An outside perspective is often helpful in assessing our giftedness.

Question 8. For those members of your group who don't have a specific "calling" that they feel they should pursue, it would be appropriate to pray that God would lead them. At the very least, encourage them to take question 9 seriously.